The stage
Lights up
The music in the milieu
Plays melodious
Alas my world…

WORDPLAY

By
Howard Parchment

Thank you for the support.
03-28-04

Copyright © 2004 by Howard Parchment

All rights reserved. No part of this book shall be reproduced or transmitted in any form or by any means, electronic, mechanical, magnetic, photographic including photocopying, recording or by any information storage and retrieval system, without prior written permission of the publisher. No patent liability is assumed with respect to the use of the information contained herein. Although every precaution has been taken in the preparation of this book, the publisher and author assume no responsibility for errors or omissions. Neither is any liability assumed for damages resulting from the use of the information contained herein.

ISBN 0-7414-1791-X

Published by:

519 West Lancaster Avenue
Haverford, PA 19041-1413
Info@buybooksontheweb.com
www.buybooksontheweb.com
Toll-free (877) BUY BOOK
Local Phone (610) 520-2500
Fax (610) 519-0261

Printed in the United States of America

Printed on Recycled Paper

Published December 2003

WORDPLAY

Contents

Foreword	i
Something New	2
This Morning	3
My Universe	6
I Believe	7
The Limit	9
Life Should Be	10
The Hunt	12
The Quest	16
Now	17
Mother	18
The Game	19
Gods of Love	22
Immortalized	25
My Type	28
Mesmerized	29
An Angel	32
Entangled	36
A Formula for Success	38
Thank You	41

Foreword

When Howard first asked me to write an introduction to his book, the excitement soon left room for anxiety. I soon realized that the task was not going to be an easy one. I wanted to make sure that I had the necessary tools to grasp and present Howard's essence in this foreword. After all the discussions that I had the privilege to share with Howard, it was still difficult for me to fully appreciate his conception of life as well as his deepest beliefs. It is through my acquaintance with his writing that I was able to pin point the full extent of his vision and his conception about life, love, relationships and human nature.

Understanding Howard's vision is essential to fully appreciate the following work. This is where my anxiety rose. I feel that I bear a great responsibility: encompassing his vision in a couple of pages is not only pretentious but also impossible. Yet, the process is essential to make the best out of this reading experience. I am being trapped between the impossible and the necessary.

The difficulty presented to me here are in two folds: first, I need to be faithful to the author by summarizing his philosophy and vision in a few lines; then, I need to restrain myself not to give a narrow interpretation, leaving every reader touched differently, gathering what is pertinent to them.

The first concept that can be extirpated from the author's work is the influence of the milieu on one's individuality. Everything that surrounds us has an effect on our life and our conception of it. The first and most important source of influence that one faces is family. Its importance for Howard is deeply represented in his poems. You can feel that this is where he got his roots and part of his inspiration.

His profound awareness of what is around him led to further his inquiry of the subject.

As a result, the author defines individuality as an extension of one's universe. Starting off with family he soon makes us look around to find friends, enemies, love, hate... All of these being part of this environment are so essential to define and fulfill our individuality. Once somebody realizes the influence that his surroundings have on him, only then can he live in harmony, accepting the positive while pushing away the negative?

An individual, according to this belief is not seen as a unit but rather as an amalgam of the different components of his environment, a mirror that reflects what is around.

One can choose what aspects of his environment will predominate in his personality. Therefore the only things that can stop somebody are the choices that he makes. The only limit that one has is oneself; one should first define his universe and live according to its rules, assuming his choices. By conceptualizing our environment as being malleable, the author suggests one's responsibility Vis à Vis the situations he faces, whether good or bad.

Our mind takes control over what is around us: people, nature, and events. Being able to truly appreciate one's environment is to accept the limitlessness of one's mind, stopping to be victim of it.

I do not wish to mislead readers into believing that all the answers about such a complete subject are given in the following pages, rather it gives a new perspective to old questions: what affects us and in what ways? Which part of us is enslaved by society and how does it affect our true nature? How can one define his limits? This work provokes reflec-

tions because the author uses poetry to ask questions rather than trying to answer them.

The philosophy put forth by the author allows going above and beyond one's limits. Yet, an important part of this philosophy would not be possible without the notion required by greatness, passion. Passion here is closely associated with love, love broadly defined and gradated from its most basic and essential form to its highest and universal one.

Love in its most essential form is love towards oneself. Without this basic notion love cannot exist. This definition really puts things into perspective: love towards somebody else cannot be materialized if lovers do not love themselves in the first place. Love has a spillover effect: it flows out once one is completely satisfied with it. Loving one's self is the hardest love of all. Yet, as it was said earlier, we are the reflection of our surrounding, therefore learning to love ourselves means learning to love what is around us and vice versa. Through Howard's poetry narcissism makes room for the belief that love is universal even when directed towards oneself. Actually, he makes us understand that it is essential for one's well being and evolution.

Love for others can then grow true once it has taken strong roots in one's heart and soul. It fulfils us as human beings because loneliness is dreadful. One cannot exist without the tie that love creates between oneself and the rest of the world. Therefore love has first this intrinsic component then it needs to develop and reach towards others, in particular "the" significant other. Many of Howard's poems express this search: sometimes happy, others sad, sometimes selfish, but most of the time altruist. This quest takes many forms; it hides behind a look, a gesture, in brief moments that seem endless. One forgets himself to the other.

Finally, when you realize what you have and can appreciate it, you realize how fragile a relationship is and its value.

Love as broadly defined becomes a metaphor for human nature. Indeed, Howard explores and expresses his deepest convictions about human beings. In fact human beings are defined by love, either by it or the lack of it. Human beings are defined through the different gradation between these two extremes. Therefore love becomes a measure. It makes us, it may destroy us and it even has the power to immortalize us.

Love never dies, it lasts forever. Even in brief moments of passion love stains the people that it touches. Something always stays even if loves goes away: it immortalizes short moments one after the other. But what is love, really? It is about beauty, accepting the other as oneself, communication, understanding, and action. Love is about what you want to make out of it. It is everything and anything. Love defines us as human beings; it brings out our true nature denuded from social dogmas and pressure.

This is why it is divine in nature. It is as close as people will ever reach to God. Indeed, nobody possesses love rather people are possessed by it. It is an encompassing force that encloses all things.

Howard completes his reflection by reminding us of the dual relationship in everything that surrounds us. Our environment has an incidence on us just as we have an effect on it. Love obeys the same principle. We determine how we are going to love but love is not passive, once one possesses it he is being controlled by it. This is the dual reality of things expressed in Howard Parchment's work.

I could not conclude without addressing what I think is the biggest success of his work. Howard is a man with a vision, as the next few pages will reveal. He brings people together to make them realize greater things that they could have done on their own. He brings worlds together, and he has done so for as long as I have known him. He elevates people to see further and expands their horizons. In the case of this book, he is faithful to his tradition, he makes the world of poetry and the worlds of the streets collide. By doing so he seeks to open minds revealing to one another what each has. If this book has one success it is to make people see through different lenses and assess themselves from it.

Jean-Phillipe Noel

Something New

I have something
New to say
I love wordplay
But don't
Waste my time
Saying something
Spiritless
You left me
Cold in effect
Search within
What do you
Feel there?
I want to peer
In your eyes
And see fire

Build a bridge
Talk it
Like you live
I see you watch
From the side
To customize
An image
For the public eye
Unlike the weather
I never change
When you see me
Remember
I alone
Judge me
So be true
Something's new

This Morning

I woke up
This morning
Burdened
By living
I am lying
In my bed
Looking
At a gray ceiling
Trying to find out
What I'm feeling
I remember
It was what
I forced myself
To forget today
During
Painful yesterday
It reminds me
Of the first time
We met
Except
This time
I'm unhappy
My heart carries
A cargo
Laden with sorrow
Dissect it
Call it
What you will
There are
So many
Fake people around
You probably
Think it's cool
To disbelieve

I have no regrets
I'm happy we met
And every time
I skip through
The photo album

In my head
I remember
The good times
I lay
In the bed
Of mistakes
That I made

If you had
Asked me
To bet
I'd lose
I never thought
It would come
To this
I took for granted
Until
It was too late
My most intimate moment
Was a kiss
Am I man enough?
Something so simple
Meaning so much
If I could turn back time
Do you think
I would?
Then I'd never know
I had it
So good

My Universe

Everyone
Has the right
To be happy
I am devoted
To my happiness
In my boundless
Universe
There is
No consequence
I alter
My course
To how I
Really feel
There is
A limit
The heat rises
The pot sits red
Softly whispering
I am accepted
By those
Who like me
The rest
They have to
Remain tolerant
Of their own
Narrow-mindedness

I Believe

I believe in me
And love I have
For which
I do things
I don't care
What you think
I will not question
My beliefs
I believe
In my good heart
It does good things
I love me
I love all
That I have done for me
I love my family
They stand behind me
I love everyone
Who believes in me
I love my life
I would not change it
For anything
I love my brother
There is none
Greater than me
And I will not
Fool myself
To think
That I am better
Than another

I have enormous
Potential
I can do anything
I put my mind to
There is no limit
My mind
Is like no other
The physical shape

Of my mind
Stares you
In the face
My mind is great
I am great
My soul lives forever
I love Mother Nature
And her relentless drive
Rain may spoil the day
But there is
A bright side

The Limit

I was rich
And had a huge
Family
To take
Care of me
I am
Assimilated
My family
Dissolved

They are
Self-involved
The youth
Is exploited
There is
No respect
It is survival
Of the fittest
Hatred is fed
Through fear
Here
Dreams
Are stifled
Seeds
Of Mediocrity
Are sown
Thick

I was raised
By role models
Who grew up
Like me
They taught me
Not to lose
My wits
The sky
Is the limit

Life Should Be

Life should be
About peace
The people stop deal
No nonsense
The nation strong
No weak fence
Escape in a book
No crack house ends
Physical fitness
Sets new trends
No cigarette
To fog up my glass
Face up to things
No matter
What happens

Don't hassle
To buy death
In a bottle
It makes you hyper
And your brain rattles
To drive drunk
And end up
In a shackle
You're fighting
A loosing battle

Don't worship green
Nor sell out
To big dreams
At nights
I hear
The lost souls scream
Burn in hell
Why you
Had been so mean

You live
In a big house
Is that real?
You sold out
To the devil
Your soul him steal
Wasting your time
Not knowing
How life feels

Teach others
It don't matter
How often
Lay it on thick
You don't need
A balling degree
Ask God
"Please
Forgive me?
I was lost
Not knowing
What life
Should be"

The Hunt

The day plays host
To 38° degrees
Humidity joins in
As the sun dances
Over the hunting ground
The hunter patrols
Alert eyed
The thrill of the hunt
He scans
The savanna

It's day two
Of the hunt
And
He is prepared
Escape routes
Are mined
By traps
With protruding spikes
He holds a net

His objective
Is to tire his prey
And when
It is overwhelmed
Cast his net
To capture it
Before
It recuperates
Speed
Strength
And cunning
Will determine
Its fate

The sun sets
Positioning
To the west

The prey circles
Then approaches
Eyes are fixed on it
It lifts its head
Aware
Of his presence

The hunter emerges
From the bush
The prey flees
Walls of spikes
Deny passage
Failing
Its flight
The prey turns
Heart-racing
Faster than
A timekeeper's watch
Some yards
From the hunter
There is an escape
That is unblocked
Their eyes
Make contact

A race begins
To reach
The cut off point
A sense
Of fierce danger
Fills the air
They approach fast
A second behind
Will ruin the day
For the hunter
Or the prey

A moment
Of silence
Captures the two
Followed by
A loud smash
The hunter lies

Face down
As his prey flees
Without
A scratch

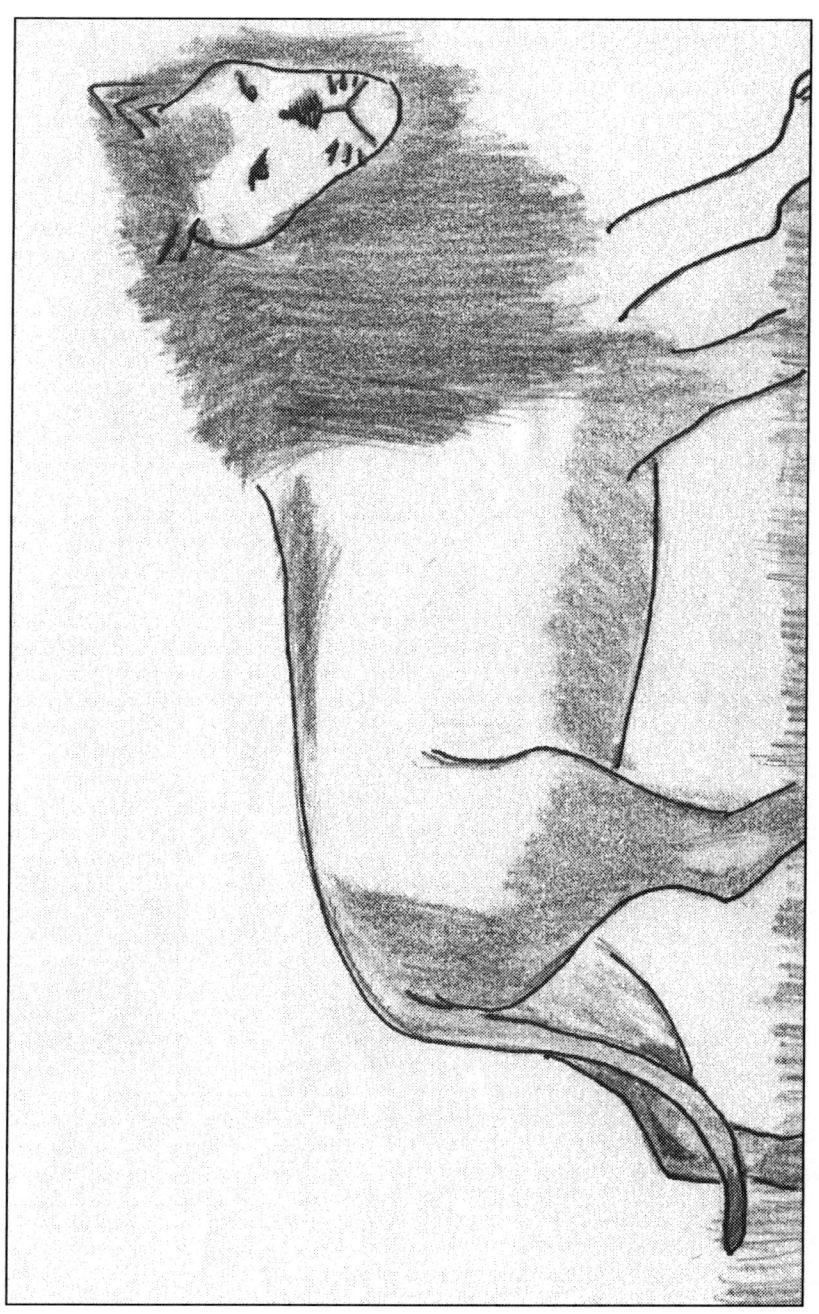

The Quest

My heart morns
So I went back
On the quest
The journey
And the rest
Contemplating
My actions
"What did
I do wrong?"
I assume
Going back
Won't change
The fact
That
I came with
Something
And when you left
It lacked
You had my heart
And still
Though we're apart
Truelove
Don't love me
Hence alone
I stand
In the battle
For your hand

Now

I am not the guy
I used to be
I am worse now
I am sensitive
Love fills the air
I care
More now
I discovered
New things
About you
Lover's leap
Is steep
Approaching
The ground
I anticipate
The fall down

The first thought
Was a vow
To hold on
Hoping
You'd
Hang around
Communication
Is fun
I understand
Someone
I not only
Think of myself
I think of
This person

A great thinker
A good
Human being
With inner beauty
All in one
In comparison
There is none

Mother

Born of strong heritage
Challenger of wrongs
Protector of right
Stare at the stars
With wonder
And delight
It is you
Who inspire people
To feel happy
Uncompromising
In ways
You showed me
How to behave
I see your heart
Grow
With all its might
In essence
You made
The difference

The Game

I want to touch
My ladies' lips
Today
She says that
The next
She is on this
My woman wants
To prove me
Wrong
So
I told her
"I'm gone"
She called it
A game
I laughed
When
She made
The claim
That laugh
Turned into pain
In the end
I drew near again

I want to feel
My heart's hair
It's not so much
Her hair
It is how
She acts in it
I'm not rude
But she puts me
In my shoes
About her hair
I pulled it
In a love session
A little cunning
Regression

My lady
Drives me crazy
But I am happy
And when
Our lips touch
Lust meets
Undying love

Gods of Love

My mind
Is focused
On someone
Unique
She is the one
For this man
I remember
Having a dream
About this
Supreme being
I
The god of love
Cupid
In my dream
And Venus
Made a team
He discovers
His weakness
And refuses
To fear
Venus
Without being aware
Forsakes him
Her stare
A sight to witness
If ever
The day
Was other
Than this
He would fall
Into the abyss

He pictures
Losing himself
In the glare
Of her brown hair

Or blinded
By her stare
He fears
Pleasure
Making
The innermost parts
Of his being quiver
Her smooth skin
Made the earth
Under him
Shiver
I knew
And came
To his rescue
Tossing
Too and fro
In the dark
She left
Her mark

My dream
At its height
Tears glow
To my room's
Neon-light
Love died
A thousand deaths
And relives
So that
Venus will realize
The look
In his eyes
Cupid is reborn
Tonight
When it's done right
Cupid and Venus
Will reunite

Immortalized

The immortalization
Of a moment
Was when
Two worlds collide
One had strength
Power
Aggressive in features
And faculties
The other
Equally awesome
Had a passive
Aggressive nature
And you might ask
Yourself
"How it came to be?"
They were drifting
When attraction
Pulled them in

Emotions stirred
Heights of energy grew
In the immortalization
Of a moment
Sparks flew
The clash
To a bystander
Seemed like
Two bodies of mass
Locked
In a savage battle
With outpours
In-between
A creation of confusion
Variations of movement
Spawned
What seemed to be
A river

That dripped
Then disappeared
Into darkness

The immortalization
Is a smooth sensory
That leaves
A tingling feeling
From hands to feet
Love
Is the accompanied
Sensation
For a scene
So sweet
The moment gave birth
To a new universe
Acquiring
The strongest
Characteristics
Of the two
I was immortalized
So were you

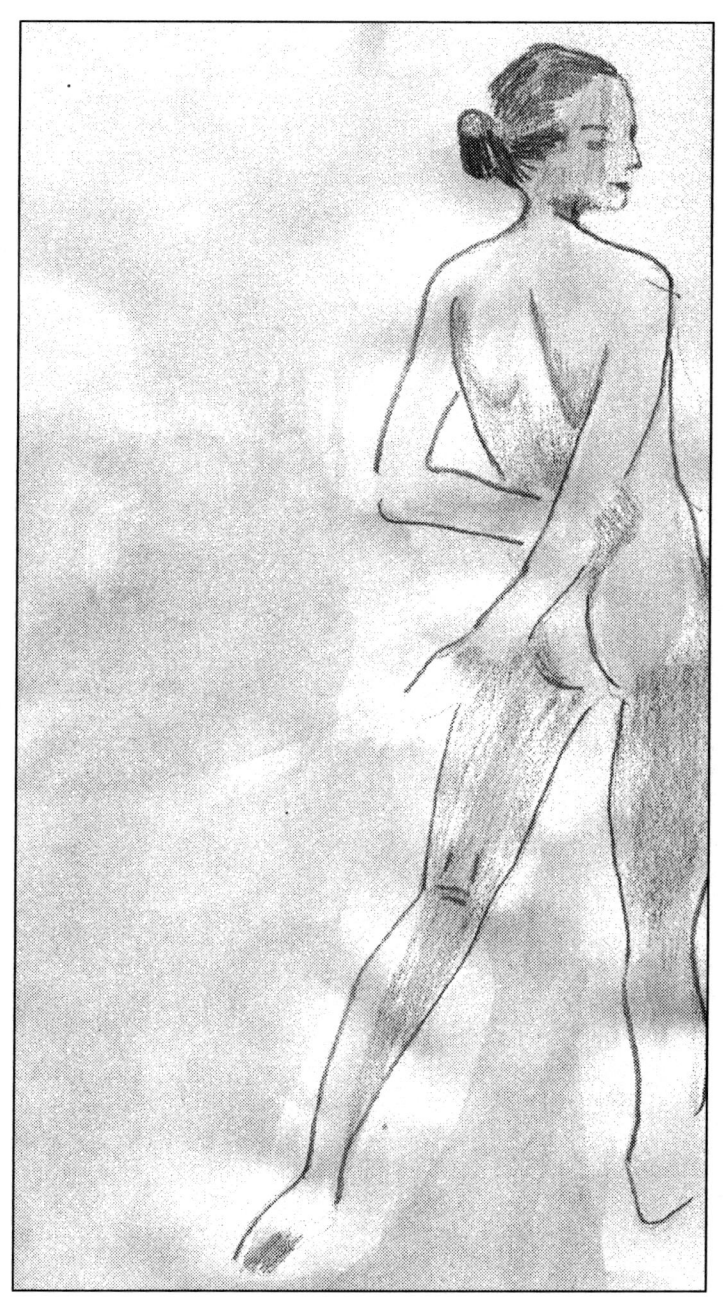

My Type

I imagine you walking
Being greeted
With smiles
Little kids shout
"That's my friend"
They run towards you
You put a smile
On sad faces
"She is nice"
My type is
Like a silhouette
In each step
A rhythm beats
Inviting harmony

I remember
I was on the corner
When she walked by
I had to try
Something
"Hi what's happening?"
"Nothing"
It was special
A morning in spring
With my eyes closed
As the sun climbs
The horizon

She shone bright
And gets
Respect
Picture
A person
Drawn to kids
With whom
A man will live
Sure of herself
And not easily
Influenced
That's my type

Mesmerized

I was mesmerized
I felt
My spirit ascend
I was in a dream
Where
A free spirit
Bounded me
With her smile
Her eyes
And her dress

It looked like
It was sewn
On her
It flowed like
No other
When we
Touched
It felt like
There was nothing
Between us

My eyes traveled
A thousand times
The uncharted parts
Of her flawless body
I closed my eyes
As her scent floated
On the wind
I detected
A sweetness
And a sweeter
Scent hidden
A vision

Of beauty
My spirit shouted
Love
In an ancient
Language
Secretly
I wanted her
To myself
In my head
I kissed
Her hand
As I asked
"Would you like
A swig?"

I think
I wanted
To write her
A book
So
She could see
Love stacked
In paragraphs
To look
Smile
And laugh
At how
My heart leapt
I felt her
Unlike anyone else

An Angel

An angel
Revealed herself
To me
She was not too tall
And beautiful
As can be
Her eyes left me
In a dreamer's trance
I stared like
I was not aware
Of the world
Around me
She smiled
With me
Her glare
Sent arrows
Through my heart
Quickly

Her skin possessed
A smoothness
That tantalized
I shook her hand
Saying hello
Not wanting
To let go
Her lips harbored
A beautiful smile
I stared at her
As she spoke
And although
I did not hear
I pretended
I heard clear
While she talked
Her bourgeois
Accented voice
Provoked a thought

That sent me
To the heavens
Wishing

Our encounter played
Over and over
In my head
I hated
Seeing her
Walk away
I stood there
Watching
Her
Leisurely paced
She turns away
From our embrace
I watched my hands
Leave her body
As they trembled
For daylight
My head shifted
From my hands
Back to the
Bloom of Beauty
And wished
I were the clothes
Close to her physique

A lot will grin
Thinking
It was physical thing
She made me
Search in my soul
To create
She stimulated me
Mentally
Is stimulate the word
When you can't eat
Or sleep
Without

Thinking of the person?
And the words said
Are repeated
To find
The wrong one spoken
So the next occasion
I will get a token
Of appreciation
Considering
I was considerate
To retrace my steps
So nothing
Goes wrong
Another kiss
A hug
Or will she comment
On how selfish
I was?

Entangled

I want to take a voyage
On a thought
So I can
Be with you
Like the sky
Without the sun
My life is dark
Without you

I want to take a voyage
On a thought
So when I thirst
Your touch
I reach out
And caress your hand
I am at peace
You rescued me

I want to take a voyage
On a thought
When I miss you
I will move a mountain
And put you on it
So I can see you
From a distance
My soul soars
Over vast territories
Entangled
In your mystique

When I want
To be with you
I reach for your hand
I am compelled
To tell you
About the desire
In my soul
To vanquish time

And space
I feel my place
Is with you
I cry out
To the heavens
And look down
To the ground
I miss you

A Formula for Success

In every human being, there lives the desire to find someone to spend the rest of their lives with. Someone that will know you inside out. A person to give laughter when sad. In times of grief that person will provide comfort. This special someone will love you even when youth slips away. You will grow old together as partners in a relationship. The search for the perfect one for some is never realized. The reason why most of these encounters don't work is because one or both partners are not getting what they are looking for from the other person.

There are many different kinds of successful relationships. Most relationships have a similar formula for success. I will focus on the most common relationship, which is called an equal partnership. An equal partnership is when each partner assumes equal responsibility in the relationship. It is a shared effort where the pair joins together to build an unbreakable bond. A bond that will withstand the blows of life. A partnership requires time and attention. Partners at times are distracted from their tasks, consequently disappointing the other mate. An equal partnership is a difficult endeavor. Most equal partnerships attribute their success to love, communication and commitment. Once these elements are present happiness is eminent.

There are different kinds of love. The love found in an equal partnership is called the unconditional love. This kind of love conquers all. When people are in love it holds them together through the good times and the bad times. Love is essential for a successful equal partnership. "No one is an island" is used as a proverb explaining that people are not meant to be alone, as one songwriter puts it "everyone needs somebody to love." Unconditional love is the fundamental emotion shared by both partners in a relationship. It is a splendid feeling to be in love.

A partnership needs constant nurturing for the love to endure because life presents situations that will test the couple's love for each other. As another songwriter says "life is one big road

with a lot of signs." Love is a hard feeling to describe. Some say love fills you up with joy for example, waking up in the morning in a bad mood and the thought of your mate puts you back in a good mood. Unconditional love fuels partners to excel and grow.

In my opinion, love is best described in actions. People say love can make you do crazy things. The actions that are portrayed through unconditional love are for instance, surprising your lover by making their favorite breakfast. It is as the saying goes; if you love a bird you can let it fly away and if it loves you it will return. The moral of the story is that love is not controlled. Love is fostered. Unconditional love is thinking from the heart. Happiness can be achieved by following one's heart. To ensure that the pair stays happy communication is vital.

Communication in an equal partnership is to express one's self verbally and/or visually to one's partner. Open communication is imperative in a successful equal partnership. People are different so for them to remain happy they have to communicate fully and freely with each other. A better understanding of the other partner will flourish with good communication in the relationship. The couple can communicate what they are looking for from each other. In so doing, they can know each other's likes and dislikes thus creating understanding. Open communication in the partnership is expressing when one is troubled and when one is happy. The partner is then able to assess the situation to find an agreeable approach.

A relationship with open communication pulls the couple together. The better they know each other, the closer they will be. It creates a shared ownership. The pair is in it together on a winning team. Both partners talk about things and work them out together thus favoring trust. As a result, there will be fewer problems as the couple gets closer. They can concentrate on one another. The pair can focus on having fun. This enables them to bring the partnership to higher levels of intensity. A mate who does not put a hundred percent effort into communicating with their respective partner will have difficulty keeping their love alive. A lack of communication is usually attributed to a lack of commitment in the relationship.

Commitment within the pair is when both partners are at the stage where they realize that they have a good thing going. The couple decides they have found what they are looking for from their partner. They have something worth holding on to. The pair forms a union of love and understanding. They vow to be there for each other in times of crisis. Committed partners support each others' endeavors in an equal partnership. The couple takes an interest in the other mates' ambitions. In so doing, they can offer advice and/or help. In my opinion, committing to your mate is saying "till death do us part. " The comparison is to highlight the rule of commitment which is; nothing is allowed to interfere with the couple's happiness.

Commitment is a serious step for both partners. It requires partners to make sacrifices. The priorities are changed in a committed relationship. The couple takes a higher stage of importance in the partnership. The pair's primary focus becomes the relationship. They plan and build their future together. Each positive step in a committed partnership strengthens the couple's bond.

A committed equal partnership will stay unbent by the burdens of life. Over time, as the relationship gains momentum nothing will stand in the way of the couple's happiness.

The possibility of finding someone and living happily ever after still exists today. The times have changed but relationships remain the same. There are simply more distractions in today's society. People are building successful partnerships. Of these partnerships, an equal partnership is the most common. They are finding unconditional love through understanding of each other. There are couples who have achieved new levels of understanding because they communicate openly. In so doing, they have fortified their trust. Open communication has broken new ground favoring each partner's commitment in the relationship. Committed, the pair is an unstoppable force that will stand the test of time.

Thank You

First and foremost
I want to thank the Almighty God
Who makes all things possible
For the talent to write this book
To my Grand Parents,
Thank you for the love and knowledge
That you have past on to me
To my parents, I pay tribute
For your hard work and sacrifices
Also for reminding me what you expect
And always telling me to plan ahead
To my brothers and sisters
I hold you close to my heart
I strive to make you proud of me
A special thanks to my Aunts and Uncles
For their nurturing and advice
To my cousins, unity has help us
To overcome life's troubles
Thank you Patrice and Monique Walters
For always putting me on the right path
To my relatives and In-laws
I love you all.

Thank you to Rev. Darryl Gray
For reminding me to get the job done
To Mark Odle, David Austin,
Rosetta Cadogan and Debbie Young
Who were my mentors
Thank you to my teachers
For believing even when I did not listen
To the parents of my friends
Thank you for making me feel special
A special thanks to Irmeli Francis
Christine Althey and Jean-Phillipe Noel
For endorsing my book

To everyone I hassled
To read my pieces
Thank you for your patience
I am grateful special thanks
Rohan Barrett, Dwayne nelson,
Jerome James, Carey Anderson
Alexis Cambridge, Terrian Cleighorn
Norman Moore, Kevin Cole
Carrie Armistead, Tramaine Burke
Swancy Blaize, Vanessa Eloi
Rose-Judith Mathieu, Michael-Dean Di Rocco
Donna Newman, Shanice Moody
Fredo Jean, Lloyd Forrester, Jerry Alexandre
Kerry-Ann Busreth, Fannie Belanger
Abdou Ly, Mira Kehar
Magalie Pauleus, Waldemar Pawlowicz
Mireille Trudel, Arlene Lewis
Sherri Latimore, Aileen Mcalla
Tanisha Collins, Nola Solorzano
Camille Simpson, Kizzy Gill, Shakirah Taylor
Corrine Jean-Louis, Shaunet Tenant
Annie Frappier, Cynthia Delpe
Tania Woolcock, Kevin Grant
Lisa Stewart, Emmanuella Souverain
Suleikha Yusef, Bonnie Charles...
The list goes on
For everyone
Who love my book
I am indebted to you

Love
Peace
And my best wishes